PORTUGAL
Colouring Book For Kids
With Interesting Facts

D1212418

FOLLOW US ON SOCIAL MEDIA

 @grantpublishingltd

GRANT
PUBLISHING

This Book Belongs To

_____

CHECK OUT OUR

COLORING BOOK

RANGE

Visit our website for more

www.grantpublishingltd.com

INTRODUCTION

Allow your creativity and imagination to run wild with this awesome coloring book. Bring these exciting illustrations to life while learning lots of awesome facts about Portugal!

TIPS

- Don't worry if you go over the lines!
- Coloring pencils will work best, but you can also use crayons and pens to color
- Share your work with friends!
- Have fun, fun and more fun!

PORTUGAL

CONTINENT

Portugal is a **coun**try in the continent of Europe.

NAME

Portugal is officially the Portuguese Republic.

COUNTRY

Portugal is situated in Southwestern Europe.

COUNTRY

Portugal shares borders with Spain.

COUNTRY

Portugal is located on the Iberian Peninsula.

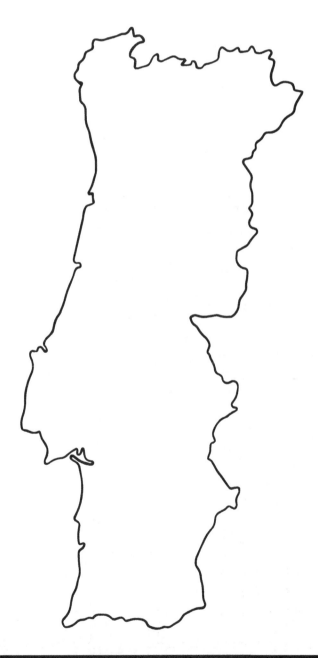

CAPITAL

Lisbon is the capital city of Portugal.

CAPITAL

Lisbon is also the largest city in Portugal.

CITIES

The second largest city in Portugal is Porto.

SIZE

Portugal is 92,212 square kilometres.

POPULATION

Portugal has a population of over 10 million people.

POPULATION

Portugal is the 92nd most populous country in the world.

PEOPLE

People from Portugal are called Portuguese.

LANGUAGE

The official language of Portugal is Portuguese.

receber
(welcome)

ANTHEM

The national anthem is 'A Portuguesa' which means 'The Portuguese' in English.

CURRENCY

The currency is the Euro.

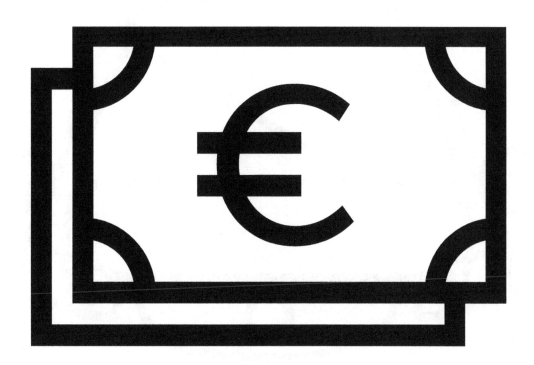

ROADS

In Portugal, people drive on the right side of the road.

MOTTO

The motto of Portugal is 'Esta é a ditosa Pátria minha amada' which means This is my blissful beloved homeland'.

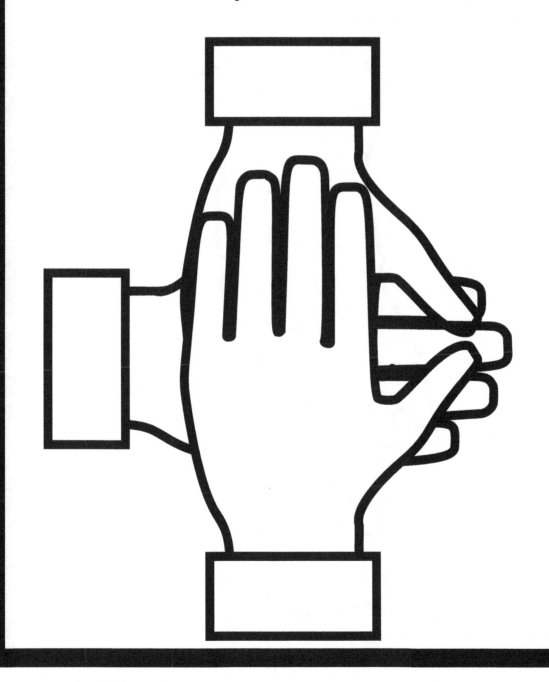

HISTORY

Portugal is the oldest continuously existing nation on the Iberian Peninsula.

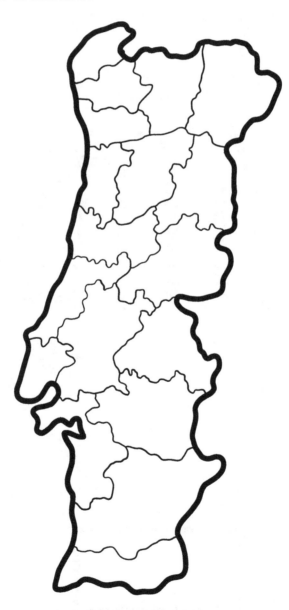

HISTORY

The Kingdom of Portugal was first recognised in 1143.

HISTORY

In the 15th century, Portuguese explorers travelled to Africa and India.

RELIGION

Christianity is the largest religion in Portugal.

MUSIC

Portugal is famous for Fado music. The Portuguese guitar is unique to this music style.

FLAG

The national flag of Portugal is a rectangular bicolour vertically divided red-green flag with the coat of arms centred on the line between the two colours.

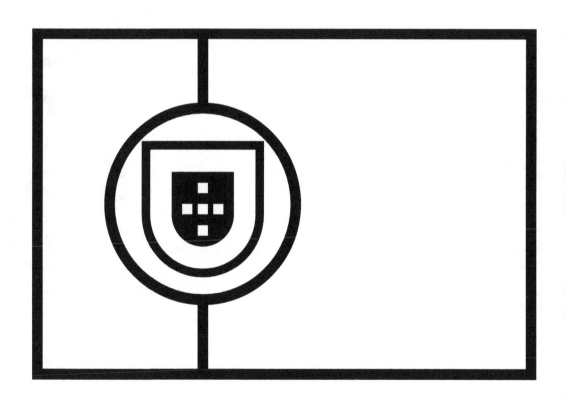

ISLANDS

Portugal comprises of its mainland and the **Atlantic** archipelagos Madeira and The Azores.

MOUNTAINS

The northern parts of Portugal are mountainous, while southern Portugal is dominated by rolling hills.

MOUNTAINS

The highest mountain in Portugal is Ponta do Pico.

RIVER

The longest river in Portugal is The Tagus River which is 626 miles long.

LAKES

The largest lake in Portugal is Lake Alqueva.

SYMBOLS

The national animal of Portugal is the Iberian Wolf.

ANIMALS

Portugal is home to a rich variety of wildlife. In Portugal there are 95 species of mammals among them are goats, rabbits, otters and flamingos.

ANIMALS

The Iberian Lynx, one the world's most endangered species, is found in Portugal.

RESOURCES

Portugal is the world's leading producer of cork products.

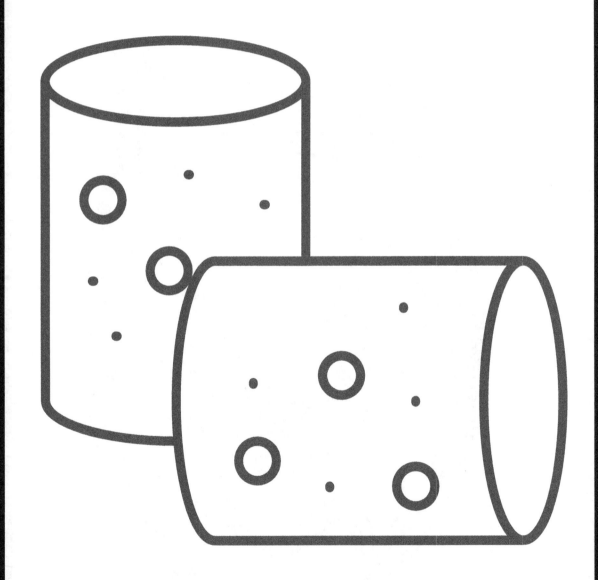

SPORTS

Football is the most popular sport in Portugal.

DISHES

Staple foods in Portugal include olive oil, garlic, onion and seafood.

DISHES

The national dish of Portugal is Bacalhau.

FRUITS

Portugal's Mediterranean climate allows for **the growth of** large amounts of fruits and vegetables am**ong them** are pears, melons, apples, plums and grapes.

THE END

Made in the USA
Middletown, DE
17 April 2023

28985492R00024